How to be a Magician

Written by Isabel Thomas
Photographed by Will Amlot

Collins

Science trickery!

It's easy to produce magic tricks if you know the science behind them.

Read the instructions carefully before your performance. Have a practice session in advance.

Get ready to fascinate your friends and family!

3

The strange straw

Instructions:

- Wrap the paper around the straw.

- Rub the paper quickly up and down the straw.

- Balance the straw on the bottle cap.

- Put your thumb near one end. The straw will move!

Required items:

- Washable plastic straw
- Scrap of newspaper
- Bottle cap

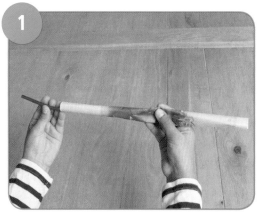

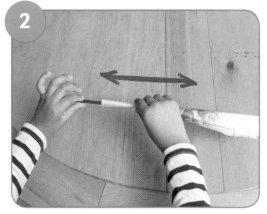

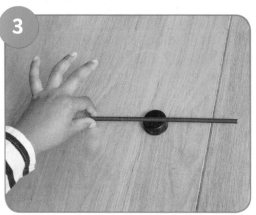

Secret science knowledge

When you rub the paper wrapper along the straw, the motion causes static electricity to collect on the straw.

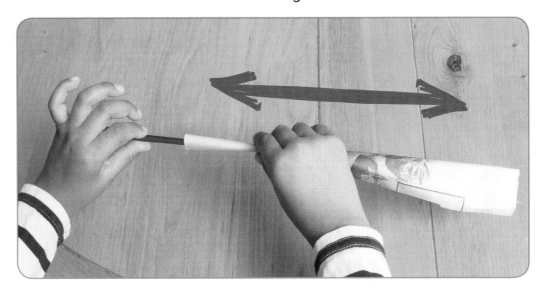

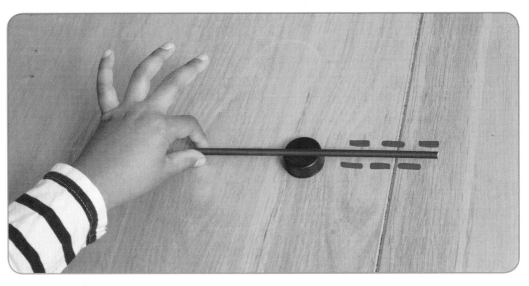

Static electricity causes the lightweight straw to move to your thumb!

Static electricity is electricity that is stuck at the surface of an object.

The paperclip hoax

Instructions:

- In advance, place a small bit of kitchen roll on the surface of the water. Flatten any wrinkles.

- Carefully place the paperclip on top.

- Push the kitchen roll gently. It will sink down.

- The paperclip stays on the surface!

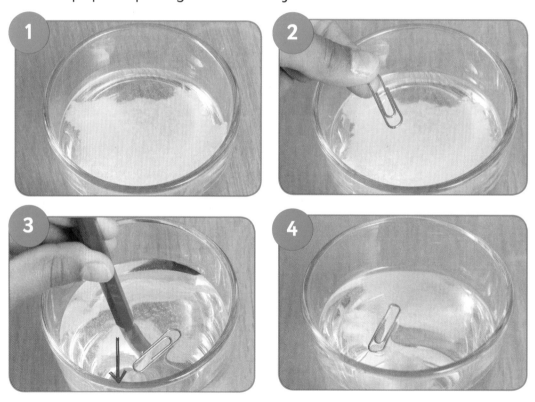

- Challenge someone to make a paperclip "float".

5

Secret science knowledge

Water is sticky! Each drop clings to nearby drops.
They cling together most strongly at the surface. This is
called surface tension.

Paperclips normally sink. The kitchen roll makes a difference. It helps the paperclip to rest on the surface without disturbing the surface tension!

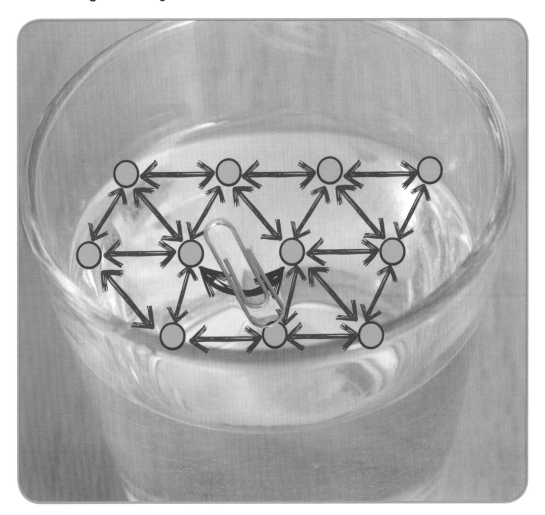

The exceptional balloon

Instructions:

- Stretch a balloon by blowing it up. Release the air.
- Measure a cup of fizzy drink into the balloon.
- Knot the balloon's neck.
- Shake the balloon.

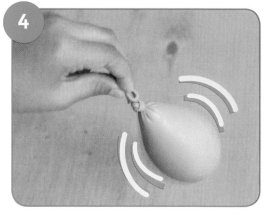

The balloon gives the impression it is blowing itself up!

Secret science knowledge

Fizzy drinks contain a gas called carbon dioxide.
Bubbles of carbon dioxide come out of the drink.
They burst in your mouth!

14

Shaking the balloon produces lots of carbon dioxide bubbles at once. Gas takes up a larger space than liquid so the stretchy balloon inflates!

The magic cylinder

Instructions:

- Assemble the magic cylinder (page 18).
- Ask someone to look at the cylinder.
- Say "Get ready!" in a loud voice.
- Flick your wrist and turn the cylinder upside down. A treasure eruption appears!

(page 18)

Required items:

- Two sheets of opaque paper
- Scrap paper
- Sticky tape
- Scissors

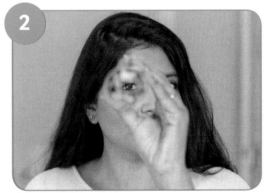

Secret science knowledge

Make the magic
cylinder by rolling
a piece of paper into
a cylinder.

Fill the secret space
between the cone and
cylinder with
paper scraps.

Roll the second sheet into a cone.

large opening

small opening

Push the cone inside the cylinder. Stick it in place.
Trim sections that poke out.

This trick is an illusion. When the large end of the cone faces people, they think they are seeing an empty cylinder!

Science is a magician's biggest secret. The second secret is practice!

Practise every step until you get the knack. Then put on a magical performance.

The tricks

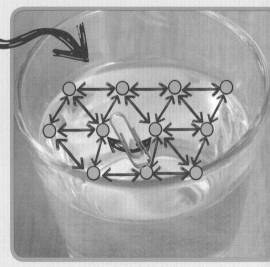

 After reading

Letters and Sounds: Phases 5–6

Word count: 498

Focus phonemes: /c/ que /sh/ ssi, ti, si, ci /zh/ s, si /m/ mb /n/ kn /s/ c, ce, sc /r/ wr

Common exception words: of, to, the, into, are, so, one, once, people, friends, move, water, any

Curriculum links: Science

National Curriculum learning objectives: Spoken language: use relevant strategies to build their vocabulary; Reading/word reading: apply phonic knowledge and skills as the route to decode words, read common exception words, noting unusual correspondences between spelling and sound and where these occur in the word; Reading/comprehension: develop pleasure in reading, motivation to read, vocabulary and understanding by discussing word meaning, linking new meanings to those already known

Developing fluency

- Your child may enjoy hearing you read the book.
- You could model reading the first set of instructions, step by step. Ask your child to read you the second set of instructions.

Phonic practice

- Help your child to practise reading words with suffixes. Ask your child to read with each of these words, firstly without and then with the suffix added:

  quick   quickly   normal   normally

  strong   strongly   gentle   gently

- Can your child think of any other words we add the suffix -ly to? (e.g. *slowly, quietly, nicely*)

Extending vocabulary

- Practise using a dictionary together to look up the following scientific terms:

  static   tension   electricity   gas   carbon dioxide

- Now practise reading words that use different ways of writing the /sh/ phoneme. Support your child as they sound talk and blend the following words.

  impression   tension   instructions   magician